SMALL ENTERPRISE

Small Enterprise

Mary Biddinger

Black
Lawrence
Press

Black
Lawrence
Press

www.blacklawrence.com

Executive Editor: Diane Goettel
Book and cover design: Amy Freels
Cover art: "Homesick" by Heidi Thoenen

ISBN: 978-1-62557-925-6

Published 2015 by Black Lawrence Press.
Printed in the United States.

This project was supported by a Literature Fellowship from the National Endowment for the Arts.

ART WORKS. | National Endowment for the Arts
arts.gov

For the cities we left behind.

CONTENTS

WISCONSIN WAS OUR CALIFORNIA

Because your days were tethered
to oversized moths, or bleeding aluminum
awnings, we could only go so far

as the train would take us. Those summers
nothing but radio and damp sheers
picketing the front window, imaginary

nuns I used to fold out of tissues.
At first I thought your body was dirty,
like cinema velvet. You had an alligator

spine in the foyer. I had to slide along
the floor to not wake your mother. Christ
himself was stationed on a plate

in the living room, painted by distant
grandfathers who earned the chin you split.
I counted the constellation of pinholes

surrounding your knee. You thought
they were charming, but you also loved
to press your cheek into the wing

of a moth, or its twin that existed inside
my body. I was a spill of trashy pearls,
not even close to fully formed.

RISK MANAGEMENT MEMO: COMMUNITY OUTREACH

At first it was like one of those riddles
they assigned to keep us busy, like soldering

the white parts on a panda, building half-
boats / half-men that could reproduce themselves

with a little encouragement. I wished for
an earthquake, and it happened in ceramics so

everything that was destroyed should've
been destroyed anyway. It was a compliment.

In Lars von Trier's version of my history
I would have occupied more than one bus seat.

But I was past the candy age, and this
was a colder sort of country, which sets its girls

loose in 305-square-foot occupancies
furnished with yesterday's dormitory regalia

and suspicious electrical outlets like
pornographic slot machines for the very small.

And the social worker has her own
heavy troubles, so it's not out of line to offer

to fix her braids in the back, or put on
a pot of coffee with a shaky West Side press

which can do other things, much like
you or me, and that's called *dimensional* by

the checklist (the mild version thereof),
and I wonder if eventually checklists become

extinct in this story, and you'll just think
hard of the only lady on earth wearing red wool

and she will start buzzing your buzzer,
which is just two wasps interlocked on the floor.

BREACH YEAR

The world does not need any more music
or teenagers. My life was not hard

so I made it hard the only way I knew
how. Someone was selling color televisions

on the street corner. I used my calligraphy
skills to trace square boxes in razor

on glossy magazine pages. I was nineteen
and had a permanent coin locker

at the bus station. Sometimes benches
smelled of bleach, like the Chinese laundry

behind our old apartment. For a few weeks
my crumpled sweaters were charming.

If you wait for a city bus long enough
it will begin to rain. I was neither the best

nor the worst, somewhere between
haunted caterpillar and sexy beginner witch

in the costume section. I was skipping all of
my classes but was not signed up.

I packed beer cans into a pillowcase, traded
imaginary bracelets for cab fare.

In some neighborhoods, I was a census
taker, not statistic. I once owned a gloomy

old saddle horse. I once had much more
black tea than I could ever drink.

ORDINARY CITIZENS

When you are taught never to taste
the merchandise, it's a pleasure trip being sent

into the night, even with parallel bags
of trash, or a full wastewater barrel, some bats

exerting their freedom in what passes
for a tree. If all you have is a fire escape, climb.

Unless you are me, which means afraid.
Is it better to pace a hot floral living room, safe,

or to throw both shoes off a roof?
I was so good at what they called *the tidying up*.

A favorite apron. Maybe I ironed it.
In my dreams I wasn't dreaming, made change

for ordinary citizens. The math didn't
terrify so much as the way customers touched

as if at a funeral, or a taxi stand in snow.
At midnight I walked my uniform past windows

displaying luminous green scarves.
You could pack one into an empty Mason jar

and light an entire block. How many
nights of bleach would it take to make enough?

They always say to work your way up,
but I wanted to drop each master key into a lake.

My friends arrived late to the party.
They were so ordinary all my wild stories died

before I could tell them. One even
brought an awkward twelve-pack of Old Style

like people would be guzzling instead
of dropping lit matches on broomstick skirts.

Somebody carried a retriever up
to the roof. Two women grappled a little, then

collapsed onto a deflated raft. Not
that I would know, of course, from below,

keeping potpourri company.
Circulating the contents of a leaky red cooler.

My freedom was somewhat like
a joke the hostess recounted involving a hen

and a runaway donkey. Maybe I was
the empty corncrib, sole wagon wheel left behind

when the hen figured how easy
it was to launch herself onto a stranger's back.

RISK MANAGEMENT MEMO: THE SERVICE INDUSTRY & YOU

Once you get over the whole "three hundred mouths
daily" hang up, work in an industrial dish room

can be much like all that sex you took for granted
back in Oklahoma, where there was little else

and even the old redbud was considered puritanical
in its seasonal desires. Or perhaps the forks

that skewer you daily are not direct and horrifying
reminders of the smallpox vaccination scar

you mistook on a man of yesteryear as his stubbing
out a blunt on his own arm. Silk screen his

likeness on all your t-shirts from 1982, and a flame
is all you need to recreate the great bowling

alley inferno that left even the most prophetic local
stoners bereft. And when you storm out

on your antepenultimate day on the line and scream
about your art, nobody knows you had any.

Except maybe Darius and his mysterious sugar bowl.
Sometimes teenagers run away and towns

hold a farewell parade with abundant paper streamers.
The man with the scar misused the term

"Rococo," but he did it playfully, like to start a fight,
so that is why you're still silk screening

his likeness on the bay window of your underpants.
There are all kinds of people you can

partially waste your life with. The woman slashing
her boyfriend's tires might have suffered

through several hundred butter pats and overdone
dover sole, or its sexual equivalent.

Sometimes it's not the force of hot water that holds
all the juice glasses in obedience.

THE YEAR IN STYLE

When I met the machine that eventually
would replace me, all I thought was
how it filled the room with sun pools
and erroneous static. We both shrugged
and then I walked to the bar with no
jacket, because why not? The place had
fish tanks in the walls, years before
anyone had figured out how to work that,
so seasoning packets and straw wrappers
bobbed at the edges. I told the bartender
I wanted to look at the ocean, even if
it was unfashionable and pedestrian
of a local to assume the role of tourist.

A month later we'd be completely
snowed under. A terrible man would
walk my names (first and last) into
an ice bank with foot stomps worthy
of an ancient vineyard or military
police hoedown. I ran twenty blocks
carrying a blender wrapped in sheets,
hence the illusion of a fleeing comet.
I was on the Broadway bus phoning
the police. I simultaneously wanted to
marry and destroy the statue of Goethe.
As a child I had called it my father.
It was too late to purchase all you can
drink tickets for the New Year. I was
the new year. No, I was even newer.

RISK MANAGEMENT MEMO: MEMBER APPRECIATION

The mushrooms were only college mushrooms.
My baton was homespun, ineffective.

Let's say somebody builds a boat from scratch.
Someone else arrives home scratched

or otherwise altered. I took in an inch or seven
along the bust line. Let's say five

and call it almost even. I wish I still had that
body, though this one knows more

important things: how many sighs in a night,
why never salt, tarantula math.

I was in love with a man because of his brick.
At this point I was made of lake.

Maybe I had stolen a sled, left my very best
cardigan on a westbound bus.

Perhaps I showed him both breasts, upside
the angriest half of his head.

He had a mind of politics, a crooked red
house with stiff chairs, shameful

blankets like a spinster. Let's say we made
the idea of a fountain feel wet.

At a certain point I stopped going to work.
Then I even stopped calling in.

BEATITUDES

So basically I was a raccoon washing the same thimble
at the edge of a creek day after day, hoping eventually

it would turn into a crystal drinking glass. My previous
life was similar, only it was a stone that I was washing

with equivalent fervor and no change. Why didn't anyone
alert me? Not even the horrid little monarchs bombarding

every corner of the vacant lot with their announcements
or the inspirational sayings you'd find in bubble letters

on the ceiling of the clinic, next to a woeful clown face
or tri-color diagram with *before* and *after* in Old English

typeface. I was the rotten windmill that had terrified me
as a child. Only I had no idea, and just kept waving arms

around like it was a wedding reception, not the map room
of the library. Walking home from school sometimes we'd

snicker at the babushkas, but were we next? Hot weather
stoop sitters never visited by their daughters, sprinkling

paprika on handkerchiefs and shaming gentlemen into
palming our elbows on the way into church? When did I

become such an undesirable blanket? The donation center
lady said maybe I would come in handy to put out grease

fires or sop up deer blood in a truck bed. But I had spent
years doing those things, and many others, without notice.

One of the articles said okay, you've missed a few stops
on the highway, but that doesn't mean you need to jump

out the car window. But then that article saved a Sandhill
Crane and discovered a woman bound up in the marsh still

alive. The article fed her water and they moved to France.
So when I attempt to distinguish the foot patters of one

mouse in the cupboard from the next, I demonstrate hope.
Or the hope for hope. Or just more unanswerable holes.

RISK MANAGEMENT MEMO: CONTINUING EDUCATION

Tonight's theme is: *you are a baby nihilist.*
Tonight even the polyester curtains are an opiate

worth banning. I'm a terrible student, victim
of harrowing perfectionism mixed with remnants

of crazy-legged wonder. Not to mention
inelegance. My renegade professor's mistakes

declared genius by an academy composed
of countless lake flies and a sinister duffel bag.

If this is the library, then I'm the only one
doing the shelving, which is fine. I know enough

numbers to enter the right bus with shoulders
thrown back like he taught me: *This is your*

mean walk, this is your into-a-lake-walk
which ends in unspeakable tragedy. Save

the lake bottom for other rocks. Don't let
anyone walk through your body, little cadet.

But the best way to learn is to disobey.
And that was the first thing he ever taught me.

NOVENA OR NEVER

An entire flock of Italian widows
in black curtains prays for me

daily. The lambs in the butcher shop
window look like upside down

chairs stacked on tables. The best
I can do is remember particulars.

I fear they are inventing fake saints
because nobody dies on a rail

of arrow fire in a waxen mantle
surrounded by poison bears just for

the sake of a few hundred women
without husbands. If the bird

in the rafters is mildly exotic, we'll
watch it. If we fear the paper bag

of pistachios is regenerating
itself in the bottom creases, we stop

sharing. The current rage is a sweet
sixteen party with edible globes

and all attendees in powdered wigs.
My cousin got a build your own

bog in her stocking. My other cousin
got a diorama of the coliseum.

When you live in a buck-tooth house
with only the newest magazines,

something akin to fire rides the circuits.
You might find yourself in a chariot.

RISK MANAGEMENT MEMO: SMALL ENTERPRISE

You wanted to open a café called
Rimbaud's Helicopter. I just kept telling
myself to *look loveable*. We watched

Apocalypse Now in two sleeping bags
zipped together incorrectly. I confessed
how I was making a bejeweled saddle

for a racehorse I would never own.
His name would be Look Loveable. He
would think about killing all the other

jockeys because I rode him so right.
And this was the only true benefit
of being small. In camp they buried me

first, then poured the curdled cider
into my hair. My mother joined in, but
only in my imagination. You wanted

to give me an outrageous hickey
and to drown yourself before turning
twenty. All my friends knew better

than to try swimming in hayfields.
I met you at the gun house. Somebody
had put new curtains up, but nothing

could take away the head-marks
on the walls. Our entire city became
a place that turned its back on coffee,

even marzipan ducklings. There's
a reason everyone loves the same
things. That reason will never be you.

TO A WRECKING BALL

They tore down the third wall of my building.
By then we were too old to know.

In my dream I swallowed a tiny metal rope.
Someone found it fifteen floors

below me, and that's no miscalculation.
In 1979 we knew how to rise.

There was a man with a leather cap called
Mister Twenty-Fifth.

Some kind of captain, he shook aerosol
cans on the fire escape.

We ignored the fire alarm, and tornado
signals pulled us to swings

or the two chains that once held a swing.
Sky of grandmother's worst

Sunday offering. Sky of textbook used
by my great-uncles, since

nothing here ever changed. I was a loop
and everyone else was, too.

We all laughed at the "historic low."
My mother purchased all

of her purses in a motel room, a vinyl
orange clutch for me.

Once we saw the news anchor outside
in a silk hood-scarf,

then without the scarf and arms full.
When I moved out

I packed a west wall with my letters
and snapshots of the old

piano-tuner, his wife's boiling pot,
my mother's shoes

tipped over in the hall, what was left
of the willow tree

that some boys tried to strip one night.
Mister Twenty-Fifth

burned the ground by the east dumpsters
that next morning, dressed

in his most ragged velour, a fedora no
witness would see again.

RISK MANAGEMENT MEMO: YOUR BEST WORK

Let's just say tonight is not the night.
You have to ask for the key and it's hooked
to a piece of wood the size of, well, and

it clacks when you cross the "lobby,"
which mostly means the suckers too drunk
to work the elevator, some couches salvaged

from your childhood mall fifteen years
earlier. And the bathroom tries to mimic
double sinks of some rich lady's house

but it doesn't succeed. You bring a piece
of paper in the bathroom with you just
so you can read it again, but you can't

read in the dark, so you tuck it down
your shirt, like you're the type who'd tuck
various items there, not a copywriter

or the person who aligns all the screws
it takes to make a train, but a version of
these same women, circa 1940, before

they lost their jobs and died, or took on
role of cautionary tale, how your own skin
would never look that way, no microphone

in your past, ever. And it's not tonight
but another when the two of you decide
to freeze as part of a bizarre pact. Or

there's just a stack of papers you call
your best work, no predicting when, how
you'll do it, the streets are full of cars

wishing they had open tops. It's Christmas
again. Everyone has lived to see it, so
you let your best work settle under the bed,

and it's one of the only normal moments
of your life, it's Christmas again, you both
have gifts, everyone is wearing shoes

and is full, there's a green pen you're
passing back and forth, the snow is high
enough to cover the ankle of boots,

modesty has completely diminished
from fashion, the bartender wears a hat
like a class act, the jukebox disappeared

and somebody is playing records,
it's an old gal in violet velveteen, leg model
back in the day, maybe more, and all

the wrong things make sense because
this is your city, it could never do you
wrong, lays its razor across your window.

CHARM SCHOOL

We used to clean up so well, then
we stopped cleaning. In the high heel
bakery they play a folk song I once

danced to in a subterranean room
filled with foam and wooden beads.
I never got the point of worry cloaks

or pilot lights, somebody crouching
beneath the furnace with a celery stalk
lit ablaze. What's more desperate

than an elegant crane submitting itself
to the will of the highway, crusts
thrown from some half-shut window?

There was a miserable midrise you
could see from the turnpike. I thought
it had been burned in a fire, but no,

that was just soot and the elements
keeping Frances and Roger locked
in an apartment filled with dripping

hosiery. Trash bags or bits of skirt
flapped from certain windows.
Old men attempted fishing nearby

in a shanty made of discarded aprons.
At least they seemed to be abandoned.
Maybe people looked at me the same way.

RISK MANAGEMENT MEMO: POSITION AVAILABLE

The yellow gold of my childhood.
Corned beef on rye with mustard
thoroughly run over by a truck,

a cartoon shark on one side,
the other a spider with enormous
breasts, in the spirit of vaudeville.

Somebody picked all the lies out
of my aunt before she died. How
did they know her elbow was not

pure titanium? All of our photos
are Queens in 1979, everybody
just waiting, like that was all

we knew how to do back then.
Clutching the awkward briefcase
my father had "found" on a bus,

in two shoes that didn't match
if you looked close. Transfer us to
Chicago and nothing changes but

the intensity of my hair. Yellow
paint we peeled in strips like
hay the golden goose would shit.

Burglary at the candy store, glass
fragments in peanut brittle,
neighbors digging another hole

at midnight, in the rippling turf
grass. I watched them with my
collection of phosphorescent stars.

MINOR GHOSTS

Someone told me I should cut grass for a living.
Perhaps all lives would be better if confined

to one singular sweeping motion. Like conducting
an orchestra that's silent, or shoveling snow

for the practice, in August, when all that batters
the hedges is a quaint shower of low-grade

longing. I had no idea that hedgehogs were dolls
and teacup patterns in countries such as

the one I found myself in. No one told me to go
elsewhere, but that didn't mean belonging.

Please don't start counting the ingredients that
comprise this particular soup. It's supposed

to be an improvisation like everything else.
The cast-iron pot can be its own sort of villager.

If we begin asking the ghosts for permission
then nobody will be left to lay down the flowers.

A CHILDREN'S STORY

One snowflake was a lantern, the other
a shellfish. They were unnatural enemies.

It took hours for the lantern to realize
its shirt was inside out. Pathetic lantern.

The shellfish wanted deeper, so patriotic.
It jumped turnstiles. Lit the cigarettes

of beautiful women who didn't know
how to smoke. One snowflake was shy

but not really. They both alleged loving
beds, believed beds were everywhere.

One snowflake hid in the red wire
beard of a dead man. The other ate

a quick brunch at the Walnut Room.
That snowflake had an old Austrian

grandfather. Who didn't have an old
Austrian grandfather in Chicago, circa

1978? Even old Austrian grandfathers
told stories of their own progenitors.

The best craftsmen could carve a cage
from an egg noodle, a spider from two

glasses of water. One granddaughter
left her tankard of water on the porch

overnight. The sky took it. Deep in
a shed, her old Austrian grandfather

whittled a kerosene lantern out of snow,
saved scraps and threw them in the lake.

RISK MANAGEMENT MEMO: STOCKHOLM SYNDROME AND YOU

I have a basket full of baby spoons, but I am full
grown. I want to smell my aunt's towels all day

but instead trudge to school in the snow, given so
many liberties. My aunt once baked me a rhubarb

crisp with a faux Liberty Bell in the middle, French
style, which meant somebody would spit or swallow

the prize. I did neither, which signified a mandate to
find my education elsewhere. My whimsy only took

me so far. Uniqueness wasn't a sport or academic
subject, though my anemia was legendary, rickets

purely fabrication. I lived in a house with a circular
window wide enough for me to slip out completely.

*

Nobody has ever tried to describe this room before
so neither will I. The paint is so thick it's like sketch

pad minus easel. You never wear a shirt. I never wear
pants or skirts, though sometimes an extra wide belt.

The heat: relentless. Sometimes you are afraid of TV.
Once caught you with a screwdriver and can of Raid.

When you cry into my hands it's like the sharp pegs
I used to drive into felt lamp shades. You drove me

around until you couldn't. I'm the one who waits in line
for dumplings now, while you pour boiling water on

the radio. How hard do I have to shake you? These
streets become their own dogs, and chain themselves.

A TASK FORCE OF ONE

Eventually we realized the world
was made of retired pasta, or concrete

ridged to mimic the grooves
in a record, back when we had records

and broke records for things
such as *most eager yet bashful heart.*

I felt like the disparate contents
of a laundry basket left outside church

but without promise of a baby.
He had thoroughly gored me, husky

ransack factory, making holes
in plus-sized school jumpers, slacks

like the tent we nicknamed
The Old Fucker, not because anyone

got lucky, but for my father
and his coarse camping vocabulary.

If I had been born a river-
bank, surely this love would be yet

another poorly engineered
vessel, awaiting baptism from dull

brunches. The lady in a pink
silk bustier pierced my ears, but left

before I opened my eyes.
I was lost meat in the garment district.

My love was the only rack
of true substance anywhere in sight.

RISK MANAGEMENT MEMO: HERE COMES YOUR MAN

Sometimes the better is worse,
but masked men still rob banks, swans
continue to terrorize small children,

and a lawyer will forever throw
his paper cup out the window at an oak
that never committed a single crime

other than paralyzing with branches
or catching fire in 1979, when torches
were so popular. And it's not your

man who holds up the burger joint
with a blue ballpoint pen, stuffs a rabbit
in his vest at the petting zoo. Yours

is too busy trying to lick every
coin in the mint, aspiring to recreate
a song by the Velvet Underground

that nobody has heard of before,
the one called *Take My Wheels Off Now*
Little Mary. And when he sings

it to you with a mouth full of blood
and teeth, you believe him, as
you always have. Your refrigerator

is filled with steaks, and somebody
has folded an angora sweater
under your childhood scarecrow doll

with half a dozen pages inside torn
from various domestic or
Russian novels. He can't help himself

from highlighting the most relevant
passages. The bartender calls
by 8:15 and you need to get him out,

or somebody like him. A green smudge
of raincoat always trembling.
Every glass lit by invisible embers.

HUMAN RESOURCES ARE LIMITED

I was dancing at a club called The Downtrodden
Pony, but not for the money. I had green
glitter and pink. The walls seethed with carpet,

cages all wire like an immigration checkpoint.
My arms resembled a tiger attack,
a ruptured cloud. Not the way I moved them

but their overall sentiment. I was a box of cotton
used to soak up a paint spill,
only with fermented lime juice instead of paint.

I did it for the sense of power that comes only
from turning yourself like a coin.
I was showing them. Sometimes I drank coffee

from a flask. One manager bought us matching
sombreros with no cover on top,
asked me to model for a gyros advertisement.

I should have been at school dissecting spiders.
The lake whipped itself, making
everyone feel uncomfortable. Later I danced

at a club named Nightmare's. I kept asking to
shake tassels for Henry Fuseli.
I longed to emerge from an oversized breadbox.

RISK MANAGEMENT MEMO: BACKSTAGE PROTOCOL

Feed your northern dog is all you can do.
They put a switch in me. My necklace was pills.
Eventually we'd all become trick smoke

and telegrams, but what about the meantime?
I was imaginary, like a hot fiancé
from New Zealand. It was easy to watch

the street from my glass box,
despite all the cash and the slips and awful
marabou scarf they handed me

wrapped in a tin sarcophagus. Ginger
Rogers might have rocked it,
but not this 183rd Street tumbleweed.

The lady next door made me
drink tea from the chipped cups of royals.
By royals she meant the men who

asked us to steady their wigs at dawn.
The pills kept everything in.
I even took pilot lessons, impaled myself

on the sharpest sugar cone
in all of Frankenmuth. Took up nursing
classes just for the ipecac.

I shoplifted lipstick the color of Benadryl.
The sky looked like whores.
My dog was the prettiest lady on the block.

OVER/UNDER

Your name was a sound that I made
when pitching the last box onto a wagon bed

and readying to go west. The apple
was so proud of its seam, in a way that spoke

of afternoons in a vault populated by wet
handkerchiefs and rotten snow,

holes, Toronto on the cusp of July,
the invention of lightning like we made it all

up. Everything looked and felt and eventually
went away mad. The fish may

have been fists, or lights. Truly I
was just another mandible to you, set of legs,

a lighter somebody dropped
backstage and later felt in the swift crevices

where back meets back meets back. Nothing
good ever happens now. I walk

with an eye over my shoulder. Sinister quick
marts. Sidewalk cafés patrons

sidle through. We spent so many
hours inventing a way to conflate ourselves

permanently, like a room packed with post-
structuralists and limited

supplies of olives. In your native language
there was nothing to rhyme

with a phrase meaning we
are meant to be together but flown apart.

RISK MANAGEMENT MEMO: LIFE IN A NORTHERN TOWN

Every house has its own barrel
for burning letters and once-cherished garments

are the best way to get that sucker
rolling on a Wednesday with nothing else urgent

enough to coax a grandmother off
her couch and to the vinyl curtains, every tree

is at risk daily, news never covers
the truly breaking things because it can't, only

we know that a bowling ball will not
crack the ice but two red bowling balls will

(however, good luck choreographing
that), like when they made us stand shoulders

touching in the darkened vagina
of the school auditorium and what were we

told to remember (Vietnam), we
were never there, though your father donned

his homemade combat gear
and brandished a tongue like rickrack, golden-

rod so pervasive in your yard
that sometimes we wanted to lose our humanity

instead of our virginity, but you
always considered yourself a frontrunner not

an incumbent, and my mouth was
never the source of anything beginning with *no.*

SHOP LOCAL

So you're the girl crossing a caged walkway
bridge over the interstate, and at first people think

you would throw your textbooks onto the road
below if you could, but you don't have any

beef with geometry, even the taste of cheap gin
has acute angles. You're going to a frame

house with mattresses on the living room floor
and green carpet that double-takes as moss.

Candle wax droplets on wallpaper. Old cross
photographs in cabinets. No grandmother

but so grandmother at the same time. Maybe
you spent summers in the twin of this house.

You could find the bathroom blindfolded, or
hustle a cup of tea to the front room before

Gram noticed the kettle had ceased its catcall.
This house has a triple-beam on the mantle,

next to dead fuses and a Hummel grandfather
figurine making tired statements about

the old days. (Are glass milk bottles the most
frustrating, or the way the children can travel

neighborhoods on their own?) This house
looks out on the highway, and the backfires

sometimes feel nostalgic, like distant pops
at Midnight Mass, not good but immune

somewhat behind stained glass and countless
babushkas. You're the girl who finally

gets to pedal down to the dollar store alone,
two quarters like armor in the well of her shoe.

FAREWELL, 1979

It only took three blows
of the sledgehammer to spiderweb

what remained of our sliding door.
Nobody was inside.

Were we ever? The heavy cable
sweaters, somebody's hair

(perhaps mine) mimicking
a Bavarian double-helix pastry.

Dissolution of our fingerprints
playing department store

window. My mannequin arm near
legendary. You were off

to captain the Ridgeview Temblors.
Victory was imminent.

Someone had coffined
your locker with rickrack and foil

but you were never cool, and I was
the sophomore who melted

every pig-leafed fern in the atrium.
Your theme song wasn't

a theme song, rather the thud
a head makes hitting the underside

of bleachers. Your flask
more majestic than the water tower

where someone had painted
Lost not Forgotten in gigantic silver

mascara letters. Sometimes
you were the flagpole. I worshiped

at every last one of your
shrines, remembered my camera.

Even when they slapped
the old house down to its knees

and zip-tied its wrists,
somehow the gutters kept clinging.

This was all before magic
was uncovered to be an astronomical

phenomenon, the way a lip
becomes a red bird against glass.

RISK MANAGEMENT MEMO: ABOVE THE LAW

Everyone I hated was named Joan
or some variation thereof, and the sky
was twice as bold. The historical mattress

museum boomed. You could even bring
frozen custard in there, and maybe
a man with a leather hat

would chase the kids a little.
My man was around ten feet tall
but still didn't have a proper job, other

than holding down a bar stool.
He was so good at it they gave him
the margarine halo of a canister lamp,

found extra sugar packets to level
his favorite table. My favorite mattress
was the one where James Brown

convinced himself that velour
was what ridged the circumference
of a frozen orange. My man turned into

a hideaway filled with perforated
finch wings and baseball cards signed by
a priest. He wore one suspender

like in a gold rush jailhouse.
They wouldn't let the felons sleep
on mattresses with springs, obviously.

The first time they booked him
somebody used an extra vigorous hose
because my man looked exhumed,

too abused to have been ransacked
by a class full of first-years.
Guards avalanched him with powder.

One day he swallowed a cleaner
meant only for pewter spoons or dice.
It took me hours to wash him out.

His feet hung so far off the edge
of the bed. A bat seizured against cups
in the kitchen. His head was split

like he was some kind of latter day
Lincoln. I wanted to wrap him
in the flag of his republic.

WE ARE GOING, WE HAVE BEEN

Every man clustered beneath the Washington Bridge
that day is now dead. Perhaps they died

while I was steadying myself on a wide marble-top
desk, in a skyscraper. We used to scrape

everything short of the sky. Surviving so some day
we can be frail pensioners rearranging

seasonal doilies. We have taken and then retaken
our vitamins. In old photographs we

appear as hungry and smudged as the times, though
they were the good times, or better

times. We burned my fiesta blanket in a barrel,
not for heat or fleas, but symbolism.

We set me straight in the luxurious back booth
of a place with lint-free napkins.

I handed my beads out to ladies and drag queens
in the park, beside a bankrupt fountain.

Men beneath the Washington Bridge predicted
the weather for tourists, always

cloudy and unstable. They were never friends.
Our train phantomed right over them.

RISK MANAGEMENT MEMO: HELLO, AFTERLIFE

So little was personal about your interior longings
or your compass. You wished it was easy

like picking out the king of the bells, or killing all
moths stuck to our daily adhesive calendar,

but instead you just swept the hair away from my
eyes, said something like *eat your potatoes*

but meant something like *we're both going to die
of interior longing*, and was there a service

to perform and rid us of it: two men in old brown
suits, a storefront church, musty goblets.

Months later and it's either you rushing me or
me rushing you to the hospital, we could

save the bracelets for next time, maybe next
time we'd be there for something better.

I would entertain you with stories of evil brine
shrimp, and you would froth about Arthur

Rimbaud, how did I grow up knowing so little
about him, we could've been the best

playmates since I always walked into briars
with bare legs and that's how he loved

his cities. He loved them desolate, blocks
of dead houses inside, so the only

flashlights they'd need would be sparks, no
dormant volcano necessary. He loved

his cities to be half concrete, no telling
which half, or maybe it was simply

the potential. You both loved your cities
more than a little bloody, blamed it on

a forest packed with the owls of our mutual
childhood. Nobody else could see

them. You took me by the hand and I let
you, a woman full of plywood

and buckshot, like the pheasant everyone
fought for and nobody ever won.

COMPANION IN HELL

My childhood was packed in slander,
dresser drawers filled with fire-wool,

centipedes in the sewers, my father
always brandishing the whipping rod

just out of eyesight. My childhood
contained all the workings of fine

horses dead centuries ago but still
bones. Sometimes they would rise

out of the river and gallop someone.
Perhaps the bloodless girl. Wood

transformed into a mushroom cove.
You could press your thumb into

her leg and the plum would stay
for an hour. Understand that our

plums were very small, and the girl
had no blood. Consider it more

of an illumination. A walk through
an ordinary suburb where nobody

died meaningfully. I was tempted
to press my finger right through

her blue eye. We will not speak of
her mouth, the way her house rang

out with stones at the beginning
of every week. Our hours were long

compared to a conventional clock.
Perhaps they were eternal. The girl

was my childhood. She let me
wrap her in a leaf the size of god.

WHAT MY BODY TAUGHT YOU

It was cold and then colder. The underbelly
of an overpass, carotid of your favorite creek,

bless me. Your hands were the gentlest.
Sometimes you weren't moving, and snow

would dare itself to cross your back.
They would never pack more than one of you

on any ark. You had enough trouble
with yourself already. Thought the doilies

were handkerchiefs. Thought there was such
thing as heavenly intervention,

or fires that kept themselves to the corners
of your studio. Your handwriting

on the back of an envelope. Midnight
burning of transaction registers, your birth

certificate, but never books or blank paper.
I had not slept outdoors before

and you pulled me inside your coat.
It smelled like the anatomy of a birch tree,

or the idea of an angel on fire. That angel
would love to torture a man like you.

CONFEDERATE SOLDIER

I was a family's house maid. The man
was a confederate soldier. Half
the house was made of glass. Herons

tried to walk right in. I had my cut
finger and other liabilities.
A thirst for other people's jewelry.

I was not born in the 60s, but still
knew the difference
between a petrified loaf of rye

and the center hall of a colonial.
Half the house was made
of teak and plywood, alternating.

The confederate soldier never left
without his musket.
That's what he called it when we

were darning socks together, or
scraping blood stains
out of functional wool pea coats.

They had a yard full of hens, but
no rooster. The woman
was made of iridescent wood beads

of anger. Two broken harmonicas
that sounded equally
dreadful. A mop perpetually trying

to make it big. Sometimes I would
break her over my knee
a little, tell her that she deserved it.

There's nothing more luxurious
than a confederate soldier
out of his frock coat. I preferred

mine the flat color of a dead photo.
I preferred mine dead,
walking across a moderately deep lake.

RISK MANAGEMENT MEMO: MAINTENANCE-FREE LIVING

At this point we may or may not have been living
on soup and apples, on a bus with lengthy

stops in neighborhoods where an occasional bullet
may or may not have landed in my lap.

And then some joke about how all this time you'd
been shooting blanks, here's a live one,

quick fold it in some ripped cloth and take it home.
Your brother's cowboy bedspread.

Frost triangles on the window above the sink.
Sick enough to conjugate verbs

so distant it may well have been another century.
I did drop the crock full of honey, or

I would have dropped the crock of honey had it
identified itself. To think, someone

once fed us both generous portions. A lady asked
me for an *ink pen* and I just glared.

You bristled at her, but really it was something
we would call your dyspepsia had we

been living in the novels we may or may not have
been charged with reading aloud

into a tape recorder. I'm blind, you said, not high.
I'm not blind, it's the light here

and the lack of it there, the way everything just
rocks and rocks, then stops.

THE ART OF FICTION

You should have better endowed
your protagonist. His foil

shivers though it's an indoor phone
booth and she is not too

drunk to dial the number inked
onto her blouse-cuff. Divorce papers

always look fake, like snow
or joy. Your protagonist's teeth

are too perfect for his mien. No
proper mountain man recites Goethe

in public. No product of Chicago
turns down a jar glass for a demitasse.

Trees were in favor of the end,
or perhaps they knew it was coming,

like the team of painters in moon
gear, your protagonist drawing upon

his exquisite education to vacate
the colonnade just in time, all sorrows

partially itemized like harpsichord keys
in a parlor of rebellious silk.

BURY THIS NOVEL TEN PACES FROM THE LAKE

There's somebody out there and we'll get him
even if we don't really want him
wearing our ugly wool sweaters, funneling

the last bit of coffee from the cracks
in the counter. It's okay to be rustic, but he
is more bramble than people. Exoskeleton

of scabbed corduroy, seven layers
to mud heaven, beginning with the red clay
of another state. But you should see

the way he cleans up, like an airplane
I once saw as a child, all neglected then pelted
with dung from the fields. And how

an old lady washed every bolt of it
with a bucket and faded blue t-shirt, lemon
dish suds. That plane never found the air again,

but this man, maybe there's just too much
left in his mouth. Or perhaps, like the aurora
borealis, he's something you can sleep away.

RISK MANAGEMENT MEMO: LIQUID, FRAGILE, POTENTIALLY HAZARDOUS

The rules were drink as fast as you can,
lose nothing, sleep on your purse and keys.

I would always be the girl with the rat
in a cardboard box on her lap. Vagrancy was

a relative term, a lost wig floating down
the bus aisle. Somebody tried installing sinks

in a row along our hallway, knowing it
was not a dry floor. Downstairs the sign read

Ring bell for an eyeful, a combination
thank you and goodbye card, like the florist

who eventually stopped allowing me
inside. I seized all the bright from begonias.

Oxygen was something serious, bowls
like the ones that danced in my peripheral.

All of the containers were open. Some
fences made me safe, others modestly kept

train cars in place. Years later perhaps
all I would remember would be the odd hours

or the silver rooftops, the way to lean
halfway into or halfway away from a flame.

REDEMPTION POEM

Somewhere between the soft rock
of my childhood summers and a bathtub

filled with Honeycrisp apples I see the cop,
flipping a shuttle of celery on its back.

I'm covered with maple syrup and ants,
or at least the sensation. This man has seen

my bare shoulders, inspected all sides
of my left arm with a flashlight. No writer,

but this man has penned my story in blue
ballpoint so uncooperative the baby

cried, and I could not stand to hush him.
Years ago, it was autumn. A train

platform where I'd dragged fifteen books.
Another century altogether, one where

the costumes were still faintly fashionable
and my body so ruined yet lovely.

I kept reminding myself to be alive,
because it was easy to forget in light so

golden you could almost spread it
on everything that needed illumination.

I sat in a candle-junked grotto with papers
and the only one I allowed to read them.

My hair filled the entire block, flash
flood style, and even I knew it would never

be better than this. But I didn't know.
Turned my head from side to side in grass,

considered it more homework than progress.
I will never send this to you, probably.

At a certain point patterns become
predictable. Call me a backslider, call

our bodies a brothel waiting to be rebuilt
with federal funds allocated only

for true disasters. I block off hours
to spend gazing into my empty hands

since once they weren't. I fill lecture
halls with words you taught me, same order,

new urgency. I'm like a clock with the time
ripped out and dismantled on a table.

A goose with a bag of cotton balls
and a vendetta against the nearest lake.

Sometimes I am pure junk, and the cop
doesn't look twice at me. Likely

he has seen half this grocery store before,
stood a lady up against a freezer wall

and made her empty her bustier of steaks.
When I left I piled all my longing

into a shallow part of the harbor,
where the deadest fish congregated

in rainbow shallows. Call me eco-critical
or prone to hysterics. In my portion

of this police report I am noted
for my clarity and graciousness, so hard

to quantify, and rare, as I am from Chicago.
In a past life, you had to talk me down

from the tree. You had to carry me back
from the lake before we drowned.

RISK MANAGEMENT MEMO: NOSTALGIA MANAGEMENT

One day we put all our birthday presents
on the same boat, then lit the fuse

which was longer than you'd think,
considering how much smaller the bottles

of orange juice had become in recent years.
I was bartending at a chicken joint

named Flounder's. You could back
your houseboat right up to it, like in Venice

where all men outlived their moustaches.
I wanted to make clothes out of

other clothes, the type widowers
were reluctant to add to the June bonfire.

I guess you could say I believed in a new
life, which was not the same

as a double life. Two powder biscuits
just kept fondling each other

in the drawer. I became self-conscious.
There was something wrong

with the way I asked the new
inhabitant of my old house to hand it over.

FOR UNKNOWN REASONS

I depart with my urgency, decorative dirndl
meant to be nailed to a restaurant wall

much like my ancestors who died to keep recipes
safe in the middle bricks. They would

be so disappointed in me. I'm just badinage, or
ruined crepuscular revelation, lipstick-

hickey on a stack of papers. *It's like signing*
a mortgage, he said to me, like that

was a comfort. It's like the first time on stage,
left shoe filled with baby teeth,

armpits a sugar fire. Nobody was surprised
when my ancestors stockpiled

even the diseased apples for their fritters.
My son eats a whole wheat tart

from the grocery store, and I have failed him.
I'm not even nice, conventionally

available, or dream-worthy. I can do well, but
not good. I once asked my father to

draw me a wooden bear. Instead he painted
an enamel jackal: lost from its mother,

swaddled in wool underthings, teetering
at the riverbank on clay stilts.

RISE OF THE NOVEL

Your novel wintered in the East Village,
a coldwater flat with inexplicable
walls. Your novel was a bag of beads.
Your novel came in the back seat
of a taxi. Your novel made grievous
errors that were the genius
errors of a second favorite carriage
horse naked in a public park
along with everyone else and no one
cared but me and my poor skirt.
Your novel was neither loose, baggy,
nor monstrous, except for one
Sunday we will not discuss but recall
often, privately. Your novel was no
Versailles. Your novel was born behind
a craft store, under your jacket,
and you tried to reveal it to somebody
but your novel was not yet ready.
Your novel was the train cry background
of all my childhoods. Your novel
was a cautionary tale in the shower
with a skimpy nylon curtain.
Your novel was the second of two films
about the continental divide.

FREEWAY

There are things I do not remember doing.
I also remember not consulting my planner.
You might think it's okay to ask the snow

but it isn't a map. I put my (minimal) trust
in an approximate calendar drawn by hand.
At some point we'll stop trusting even hands

since they are not electronic. But how to fish
then; electricity is only for a mass kill or big
mistake. Like the old man who kept his radio

in a huge bag of ice, in the bed of his pickup,
and it was winter year round, but just for us.
Everything about my zodiac was incorrect,

right down to the animal. Some people lived
in the campground all year, standing behind
trees during the inspection, sending their kids

to school with bar soap and canned beans.
How warm can a stick pile get you? I do not
remember how to make a fire out of wasted

time. A landscape never begs forgiveness
but you might if you lived here. I can't recall
which happened first: the lights going out, or

the lights going out forever. It was not
a metaphor, because even the stars snuffed
out their neighbors and then drove far away.

INVISIBLE CRANE

Too young to be in the trees
but tall enough to hold a rope
in one hand, like a milkmaid

conjures a vinyl suitcase from
miscellaneous handkerchiefs,
white ones grandmother slid

into the pockets of strangers.
Tiny embroidery of three tear-
shaped pears, or were they

grenades: please daub your
cheeks in church with the pin
ready to drop at will. One year

we kept the memory of a crane.
The teenage boy next door no
longer wandered our woods.

His parents became permanent
dark threads in the curtains.
Milk crates piled out back.

The first time you see a crane,
look away. Gaze at the grass
or stare into a damp bandana.

Better clouds hang elsewhere.
It's never the wings or eyes
but the legs that return to you.

RISK MANAGEMENT MEMO: A STAR IS BORN

I was speaking but it was mostly symbols. Toenails
the color of activated charcoal. Walls spattered

with cola or similar. You had decided to stop
imagining a chalk outline of my body on yours.

You were seeing the specialist. Even chewing gum
was verboten. I had to fashion a velvet smock

for every glass item in the house. Crystal owls
not exempt. The police wanted to know how

I'd carried you so many blocks with no gurney.
As if we had one, but I left it behind. Hell, even

your wallet stayed with us. Then the bathtub,
teakettle filled with cold water. Our record

player long broken, so I screamed the lyrics,
because after so many times you don't mess with

a formula. Wheeling you out of the hospital
in late January, they thought you were holding

an infant in your arms, but it was just your arms
and the clothes I'd jammed into a pillowcase

on our way to the train. I was the only baby
you ever had. Long ago you played quarterback,

drove the Ridgeview Temblors to victory.
Somebody etched your likeness onto a feeble

medallion. You could not say the same for most
of the inhabitants of our universe. At night

I hid the phone in a shoe box stuffed with yarn.
You were a reverse Hail Mary in the dark.

WORLD-STOPPER

I have a son, but will not give him to this world.

The violence of red maples takes the top off
a hill, then buries the hill, embosses a road upon it.

I once made a log jam of anxiety. It drifted.

Some nights I pile every stack of paper in bed
because blankets are blank and so am I.

I was never good at math, but was very good.

My prank involved daffodils in the oven, crow
wings plastered into an old aunt's hair with rain.

Two men, thoroughly stoned, ignored a sign.

In the apartment upstairs, children jackhammered
a wall with television volume and corn syrup.

The bus was raw, but we still rode it all the way.

You know what I mean. We cheated on one
bus with another bus, both odd numbers. Jealous

much? My purse was ornamental, held very little.

The purse symbolized all my tiny aspirations.
One team lost its ball, played soccer with a globe.

RISK MANAGEMENT MEMO: A DYING BREED

Undergraduates, your leader cannot be with you
but wants to be. Have you ever listened
to the album *Heart Like a Wheel*

by Linda Ronstadt? Has a particular view
of the lake been "too much" for you, pen in hand,
the off-duty lifeguard lighting tin foil

with his girlfriend and too lazy to report
your body if it happens to drift past the horizon?
It is with a heavy heart that I must convey

this message of sorrow: your leader is one
of a dying breed. This dying breed has many
grandmothers, and more bravado

than a stream of ants in an abandoned pile
of cotton candy. Our society knows
he is of a dying breed, and that is why

he was denied entrance to last night's final
train. He was not mildly hog-tied in a witch room
or subjected to the frenetic urination of two

homeless men. Your leader wasn't last seen
clutching a woman in a red wig, a gypsy cab
with broken springs, the last train buried

under eleven feet of snow—imagine!
I will circulate this hand-drawn sympathy card,
as I am an artist of some reputation.

Have you ever wanted to scream at the sky
but couldn't find it? Members of a dying breed
always know the sky from its opposite.

That's because their grandmothers
are forever flinging knitting needles on the floor
of rustic cabins in Clio, Michigan

and floating up to heaven. Hence the no
obituary. This hand-drawn sympathy card may
be the only remembrance of Lottie

or Coral, who must have loved the smell
of blown-out candles, and yearned to watch that
ropy boy climb just one more tree.

GREATEST HITS

I watch for the fourteenth time today
a video tour of my former apartment

minus its previous contents, modified
to have fewer walls, slicker hardwood.

But Chicago is nothing but wet ghosts
and that's why people like it. Greatest

hits on every corner. Where she lost her
glass eye in a deep *kir royale*. Where

he had to be packed on ice again, like
the artifacts we unearthed backstage

at the museum, without a handler's
license. It's broken down department

store windows now, another generation
of flimsy interview wear intended to

set the bull pen aflame. Avoid all
reference to Baudrillard, I repeated,

though my personal god had dressed
in his business pants and carried

his manifesto into every hotel room.
It's a wonder I fit into that apartment,

its exclusionary valences and drapes.
I wore both my cross and my uncross.

RISK MANAGEMENT MEMO: STRANGER DANGER

The best birds are little green ones that move like
fireworks. If one afternoon a shadowy, unknown

man tells you he occupied your body for half
a century, he is probably right, but don't let him

carry your books to the convenience store
and offer unsolicited advice on which sandwich

combo would best suit your insides, as if he
has been there, slid his fingers and their oversized

knuckles right into your most tender ventricles.
Some day you'll be having chili at a dumpy

local attraction and he'll appear again, maybe
with a bird in a cage, and say *baby, this pretty boy*

can't live without you, and the bird is hungry
too. And while you try to signal a police officer

on the street he'll be telling the waitress how
he is your brother and legal guardian, but never

thought twice about both plugging and pulling
the plug, maybe in the same night. For years you

vigilantly requested a hotel room five floors
up, drove through besieged neighborhoods only

before dusk, with purse clamped between
your knees, essential documents dangling within

a canvas bag like a gigantic scapular. Rain
sounds great unless it's falling inside the house.

The waitress and her manager now think
that you are the crazy one, and tack the coffees

and newspapers and novelty arrowheads
onto your tab, letting him sign the receipt in your

own pen. He's practiced the signature for
half a century now. He can't wait to get his hands

out of their gloves. The bus won't drive fast.
Your hair has never looked so much like glass.

HARD LABOR

Some days you're the coal miner
and some days you're the coal.

Other days you might be the tiny
wheels on a cart that's seldom used.

You might be the second best
lunch box that's only for emergency.

Sometimes you have to put your
clothes on while someone's sleeping.

Then, the opposite. The most you
can hope for is to become a shovel.

Because nobody buries a shovel,
and even the son of a shovel is useful.

You once saw an entire family living
inside an abandoned laundry cart.

The hardest work can be staying
warm and upright, and still blinking.

LIMITED WARRANTY

The threshold between that lady with the mice in her hair
and birds in her rucksack and your sweet ass: let's be clear

that it's getting narrower, regardless of how many times
you launder the same pair of lacy pink boy shorts, inciting

vitriol of the Polish maids who claim all the washers first
then read their magazines watching Polish soap operas

that seem mostly to be an older woman chastising a young
woman while holding a stereotypical garden vegetable

such as the onion. You can swear your way out of many
neighborhoods, but the Northwest side might as well be

Neptune. In fact, that lady with the stolen silverware in
her socks was your former neighbor, the mushroom-roof

house. You thought you would live in that neighborhood
forever with your amiable-yet-alcoholic Irish husband.

Except he drowned in a river as a boy. So now it's just all
the magazines you can subscribe to, so you don't look

like a woman who expects things and does not get them.
You look like a woman whose trash consists of countless

empty boxes! A woman who never has to bend over
except in playfulness! Who never has to dress a dummy

or count down a drawer, except to design whimsical
counted cross stitch patterns aimed at the working girl

(not that kind). And maybe you have a friend who works
the makeup counter and can get the good stuff, but

then she rings your buzzer all night. Do you know who
invented the doorbell? If it was that lady with the twine

in her sandwich, she isn't getting credit for her genius.
But she won't return herself, and neither will you,

former turnstile-slider, nasty taxi dancer, triple agent
wannabe, impersonator of all who go left and then right.

RISK MANAGEMENT MEMO: WEAR AND TEAR

I want to be new again
so I can do all the same things
again, with the bricks set back,

lawn in its last minutes, we never
think of these things leaving us
but they leave us. We know

the train we're on will end
at a log station in Wisconsin,
all of our clothes in paper bags,

only books with old covers,
forget new ones, we're staying
forever we thought, it was back

when we were magnificent, or
didn't know otherwise. The best
way was to bury ourselves in

small rocks the size of peas.
You understood why I loved
the story of stone soup, because

it was all lies, and I believed
something was nothing. Just
figure in the weight of salt

generated by one angry brow.
It's the belly of the candle
that does all the flickering.

That's not true either, please
bring back the cat that cut
my chin with her back claw.

Swing my suitcase like a warm
rifle into a lake. Who needs
a real ceiling when both parties

tuck their own limitations into
bed? Our structures already so
unsound. We could not abide

the sharp pilings of sleet
you collected in your copper
frying pan, and we both ate.

DIMINISHED RETURNS

All available ghosts were super skinny
but that also meant insubstantial in ghost-measure,

a metric tough to assess with observable
outcomes. We had to check either the fuck you or

the fuck me box, but we couldn't check
both, so basically it was another game of wasting

quarters in the fortune teller tank. Once
there was that accident with light as a feather stiff

as a board. Never do it in a stolen tent.
Never attempt it in a river because the answer may

be less palpable than you think. A letter
arrives but it's a ransom note so throw it away, or

snap a picture then return to sender, but
only if you're in the picture too, in fond clutches

of your newest lover, sprawled on some
desirable bench seat with a sheep's fleece lining.

Believe me, sheep understand absence
and not just because they are seasonally naked.

Maybe we were just missing a kitchen
witch, or an appropriate hex symbol targeted at

perpetual malaise, underachievement.
Certain ghosts are forced to keep working, even

on holidays. You know, bone business
or other holy works, pushing us under the sheets.

LORD, SOME DAY HE'S COMING BACK FOR ME

The lake plays the only note it knows,
the song called *One Lady Can Only Make*
So Many Beds, and it's in a minor key,

of course. My man wears a bone
for a belt and some day he's coming back
for me. Or at least that's what the lyrics

claim. Sure, they painted white over all
the signs, but nobody can rupture
a million pints of baby oil, wet fenders,

as much faucet needed to properly
wash an apple. One day he washed
my apple. We broke into a museum.

We stole the curator's best gems. Painted
hideous portraits of fruit that rotted
centuries earlier. You'll know him when

you see him, the song says. One minute
I will be gently paging through
an archival text, my hair in a timid

haystack, and the next I'll be naked
in the mop-room, covered in black seeds
from a host of passion fruit, telephoning

past incarnations of myself through air
and flannel. My man comes back
for me pursued by police, trailing strands

of the nylon rope he outsmarted.
Long ago he made my bed, made every
bed in the house. Made the tables

into beds. If I believed in him hard
enough he would come back for me.
One woman only has so many times left.

RISK MANAGEMENT MEMO: THE HUMAN CONDITION

So maybe we prepared for a disaster
which was actually a different disaster,
and when the shit went down we were
elsewhere, as predicted by the dog man
who pushed a shopping cart filled with
grimy papers, dispensed prescriptions
and embarrassed all the nannies or kids
on their way to public health, so I forgot
the tourniquet on my hand was a shirt
and completely voluntary, though torn
by one skilled in ambulatory medicine
if by ambulatory medicine you mean
has been delirious in multiple locations,
and kind of ironic since I was the Jesus
of our workplace (they even told me
what costume to wear) and confronting
the both of us and my tortured hand in
some vestibule, God told you to take me
(which in retrospect you misinterpreted)
to the nearest clinic, and to dispatch of
all surveillance equipment, and to cash
a check at the Jewel-Osco like homeless,
or offer me a snow cone when opposite
remedies were required, and I remember
eventually the pain went away, wet paint
in the bathroom so we cowered in there
and screamed that everything was toxic
or soon to be, and it was warm or cold
when I thought maybe this is my finest

hour, then laughed about it, dropped
my bus pass on the sidewalk, outline
of some stranger's body in the street
the way you sometimes yearn for hotel
rooms for the history, and perhaps we
changed our minds and got on a train
instead, something burning up on a roof
but not the roof, and you said *that's me*.

ACKNOWLEDGMENTS

Grateful acknowledgment is made to the editors of the following publications, where the poems below appeared, sometimes in slightly different versions or with different titles.

The Account: The Art of Fiction
The Ampersand Review: Risk Management Memo: A Dying Breed, Risk Management Memo: Above the Law, Diminished Returns
Atticus Review: Novena or Never, Charm School, Shop Local, Freeway
Bat City Review: Risk Management Memo: Position Available
Banango Street: Risk Management Memo: The Service Industry & You
Birdfeast: Risk Management Memo: Wear and Tear
Black Tongue: Lord, Some Day He's Coming Back for Me
Blood Lotus: Risk Management Memo: Hello, Afterlife
Crazyhorse: Risk Management Memo: A Star is Born
The Cossack Review: Bury this Novel Ten Paces from the Lake
The Country Dog Review: To a Wrecking Ball
Denver Quarterly: Risk Management Memo: Liquid, Fragile, Potentially Hazardous
Enchanting Verses: Hard Labor
Forklift, Ohio: Risk Management Memo: Your Best Work
Green Mountains Review: Human Resources are Limited, Risk Management Memo: Backstage Protocol
Guernica: Risk Management Memo: Continuing Education
Gulf Coast: Risk Management Memo: Small Enterprise
Interrupture: Risk Management Memo: Here Comes Your Man, Companion in Hell
jubilat: Ordinary Citizens

Kettle Blue Review: Risk Management Memo: Community Outreach, Minor Ghosts
The National Poetry Review: Rise of the Novel
Pleiades: Risk Management Memo: Stockholm Syndrome and You
Quarterly West: Risk Management Memo: Life in a Northern Town, Risk Management Memo: Stranger Danger
Redactions: World-Stopper
Revolution House: Breach Year
The Rumpus: A Children's Story
Sou'wester: A Task Force of One
Split Lip Magazine: Over/Under, Wisconsin Was Our California
TAB: Invisible Crane
Thrush Poetry Journal: Risk Management Memo: Member Appreciation, Farewell, 1979

Many thanks to the friends and colleagues who supported this project in one way or another: Julie Brooks Barbour, Patrick Chura, Sarah Dravec, Thomas Dukes, David Giffels, Susan Grimm, Steve Kistulentz, Thea Ledendecker, Erika Meitner, Michael Meyerhofer, Danielle Pafunda, Amy Peck, Bob Pope, Jessica Schantz, Austin Seip, Amy Bracken Sparks, Elizabeth Tussey, Sarah Vap, Eric Wasserman, and Brew Wilson-Battles. Special thanks, always, to Jay Robinson. Much gratitude to Black Lawrence Press, Diane Goettel, and designer Amy Freels. Tremendous gratefulness to Heidi Thoenen for the gorgeous cover photo. Much love and thanks to my parents, Patsy and Scott Biddinger, and to Eric, Gabi, and Ray.

Small Enterprise is dedicated in memory of poet John Wylam (1957–2015), the kindest of the kind, and the coolest of the cool.